PARTNERS IN HOLINESS

Guardian Angels in the Lives of the Saints

Melaine Ryther

To David, Nick, Emily, and Lucy

TABLE OF CONTENTS

INTRODUCTION

ANGELS AND SAINTS AND US

"The guardian angels are our most faithful friends, because they are with us day and night, always and everywhere."

– St. John Vianney

St. John was just one of many holy men and women throughout the ages who had a great love and appreciation for the guardian angels. When we consider all that the angels do for us, it is easy to understand why.

According to St. Thomas Aquinas, an angel takes watch over a person's body and soul at the very moment of birth. All of us, whether we are saints or sinners, believers or skeptics, have guardian angels who:

- protect us from physical and spiritual harm;
- pray for us constantly before the throne of God;
- inspire us with good thoughts;
- incline us toward virtue;
- drive away evil;
- strengthen and console us in our sufferings;
- and eagerly await our prayers so that they may help us even more.

Unfortunately, most people do not realize what powerful friends they have at their sides. St. John Bosco once lamented, "Our guardian angel's desire to help us is much greater than our desire to be helped by him."

You might wonder why our guardian angels want to help us so much. Why should they care about us at all?

It's very simple. The angels love us because they love God. Since we are all made in God's image, the angels delight in being our friends. They help us not only because God asks them to, but also because they genuinely want to, as any friend desires to help another.

St. Bernard tells us that the angels love us so fiercely that their one great desire is to see that we make it to heaven, to share in the same eternal happiness that they themselves enjoy at every given moment. In other words, the angels want us to become saints. And everything they do for us is a means to that very end.

Now, some of us need a lot more help than others to reach that goal. The road to sanctity is long, winding, and uphill. God is very much aware of how difficult this journey is for us. And that is why He gave each of us a lifelong traveling companion. *Partners in Holiness* tells the stories of nine men and women who, with the help of their guardian angels, made that journey successfully. What makes these particular saints stand out was the extraordinary nature of the "roadside help" given them by their angels.

Most of us will only see our angels after death, when our guardians will then lovingly accompany our souls to heaven or, if needed, to purgatory. But the saints in this book all had the unique privilege of seeing their angels while they were very much alive. Not only did they see them, they talked to them, laughed with them, argued, and cried with them.

Is that why they became saints then? Because angels appeared to them?

No. These holy individuals became saints because of the great love for God they carried in their hearts, and for the virtues they heroically displayed in each of their callings.

At certain junctions along the spiritual road, the angels may have lifted them over puddles, removed large boulders from their paths, or scared off frightening predators, but never did they give them a "free ride."

Nor should we expect our angels to do all the work for us during our struggles with life. But we can certainly expect plenty of help. All we need to do is ask. "Call on them and honor them frequently," St. Francis de Sales says of the angels, "and ask their help in your affairs, temporal as well as spiritual."

Our guardian angels have so much to give us! Just a thought directed their way, or a "thank you" now and then from our lips brings endless joy to them and countless graces on us.

We will probably never have the pleasure of reading at night by the light of our angel's hair, as did St. Frances of Rome. But like that great saint, each of us has an angel who loves us just as tenderly, who tends to our needs just as well, and who accompanies us always, though remaining invisible to our eyes.

May the miraculous events recorded in the lives of these blessed men and women inspire all of us to reciprocate that love and devotion for our own guardian angels, *our* partners in holiness.

"Behold, I send an angel before you, to guard you on the wayand to bring you to the place which I have prepared."

– Exodus 23:20

ST. GREGORY AND THE BEGGAR

Silvia read the letter a second time. She was not surprised that her son, Gregory, was ill. His severe fasts were well known among the religious communities in and around Rome. Silvia's convent was near the monastery of St. Andrew, where Gregory lived with his fellow monks.

If only I could tend to him myself, she thought. *I can't bear to lose him so soon after Gordianus.*

Tears welled up in her eyes at the memory of her dear husband. She recalled how after his death people she thought were her friends called her crazy for wanting to enter a convent. Why would anyone, they argued, want to trade a luxurious estate on Rome's prestigious Caelian Hill for a secluded cell in a nunnery? Silvia had not been able to answer her critics. The love she felt for Christ and her desire to dedicate the rest of her life to Him were feelings she was unable to describe.

But she never had to explain herself to Gregory. His passion to serve God, if anything, surpassed her own. The seven monasteries he founded with his inheritance money were proof of his zeal.

No, Silvia had no misgivings about leaving her wealth behind. But now she was glad that she had saved one small keepsake from all her former possessions. It was a handsome silver dish, and she knew just what she was finally going to do with it.

She rushed to the garden and picked as many fresh vegetables as she thought the dish would hold. With meticulous care, she cleaned the food and arranged it on the platter. Perhaps Gregory would smile when he saw the memento from their past life together, she thought, as she handed the platter over to a messenger. She hoped he would.

Then, turning back to the quiet solitude of the cloister, she busied herself in prayer for her son's recovery.

* * *

Gregory did eventually recover from his illness. But the damage to his body from the long fasts was irreversible and was destined to remain with him for the remainder of his life.

If that life could have been spent at St. Andrew's, Gregory would have been overjoyed, sick or not. But the reputation for administrative wizardry he had gained years before in Rome's civil government followed him like a second shadow, and it wasn't long before Pope Pelagius II called on him for his political savvy.

"You will be my envoy to the Emperor," the Pope told Gregory in the summer of 579. "Your mission is to obtain help for us against the Lombards."

Gregory knew that the Lombards, an invading Germanic tribe, were threatening to sack Rome. But what could he do, one monk against a horde? He pleaded with the Holy Father to let him remain in the monastery, but the Pope would not be swayed. Gregory's aristocratic ties could open doors at the imperial court faster than an entire corps of clerics, the Pope reasoned. And with the invaders at the gate, time was of prime importance. Obediently, Gregory traveled east.

For the next seven years, Gregory served in the royal court at Constantinople. Though he tried mightily to muster military support against the Lombards, his efforts were largely unsuccessful. The Emperor's troops were constantly engaged elsewhere, it seemed, and unable to commit to Rome. Nonetheless, Gregory did form many friendships during his stay in Constantinople that would prove valuable in the future.

Upon completing his diplomatic assignment in 586, the only future Gregory envisioned and desired was one spent back at St. Andrew's. For a short time there, within the peaceful solitude of the monastery walls, he resumed his writing and spent long hours contemplating God and His Mysteries with little distraction. For Gregory it was an idyllic life.

But God had other plans for His talented servant.

One evening as Gregory crossed the courtyard on his way to his room, he caught sight of a beggar outside the gate. Ever mindful of the good fortune he had been born into, he never failed to give what he could to the poor. He approached the man and held out his hand to put him at ease.

"Friend, what brings you here?" asked Gregory.

"I have nowhere else to go," replied the man. "I was a merchant by trade, but my goods were lost in a storm at sea. I have not eaten for days."

Gregory's heart ached at the sight and sound of the man's destitution. He reached into his pocket and took out some coins.

"Take this and get what food you can with it. Come back when you run out."

There will be many more like him, thought Gregory, as he watched the man slip off into the night. He had heard the news that floods were devastating northern Italy and would reach Rome by autumn. The city would likely be devastated.

Several months later, in the midst of the flooding he had feared, Gregory saw the same beggar again. The man looked even more pitiful than before. The Tiber had overflowed, said the beggar, destroying the granaries. There was no food to be found in the city. Gregory at once gave the man a basket of bread and vegetables. The beggar was immensely thankful.

A week later the beggar returned outside the gate. Gregory said a silent prayer of thanks that he had been the first to see the man, as some of the monks were wary of getting too close to strangers these days. Plague had hit the flood-devastated region, and people were fearful of one another.

This poor soul will surely die if he stays here, thought Gregory. *If only there was more I could do for him.* Suddenly a picture formed in Gregory's mind. Of course! He raced to his room and retrieved from his meager possessions the silver platter his mother had given him years before. He returned to the beggar.

"My friend, take this dish. It's good silver and should fetch a fair price." Then Gregory reached into his pocket and pulled out his last few coins. He forced them into the stranger's hands along with the beloved keepsake. "Now, you must leave the city. Trust in God's goodness, and He will see to your needs."

Walking back from the gate, Gregory was confident God would take care of the poor merchant. When he reached the door he looked back, but the beggar was already gone. Gregory hoped he would see the man again, in better times.

* * *

In February of 590, Pope Pelagius fell victim to the plague. Given his administrative skills and reputation for personal holiness, Gregory was the obvious choice of successor. Obvious to everyone, that is, but him. The thought of being Pope frightened him so much that he tried to flee in secret. But his plan was soon discovered. On September 3, 590, Gregory was named the sixty-third successor of Peter.

Like every other job he had been given in his life, Gregory performed his papal duties with care and diligence. His experience in civil matters soon proved invaluable when the Lombards invaded Italy and threatened Rome in 592. Through skillful negotiations, Gregory established treaties with the Lombards, and eventually his influence strengthened the Church's presence in Spain and France as well.

Though during much of his papacy Gregory acted in the role of a temporal ruler, he never forgot he was primarily a pastor. There were many people to care for in and around Rome as a result of war, pestilence, and famine. Gregory did his best to provide for them all. He made sweeping reforms in the administration of the Church's treasury and used those resources for feeding the hungry, ransoming the imprisoned, and caring for the sick and injured.

No one disputed Gregory's genius for solving problems. But an even greater trait he possessed was humility, a virtue that he himself called "the root of goodness." In no better way did he manifest this virtue than by a practice he began early in his papacy. Each day he would invite twelve poor persons into the papal quarters and serve them a meal himself, in imitation of the Last Supper. On one particular day, Gregory saw that an extra person had entered the dining area.

"Why are there thirteen guests here today?" Gregory asked his steward.

"Your Holiness, I assure you there are only the usual twelve."

"I am certain I see thirteen!" Gregory insisted. But looking around again, he saw only twelve. He shrugged and assumed that fatigue was playing tricks on his mind.

As the evening progressed, Gregory became increasingly drawn toward one of the visitors. Every time he looked at the man, it seemed he was looking into a different face. At one point the man would appear young and handsome; the next, old and noble. There was a quality about him Gregory couldn't quite place, but it was oddly familiar. Finally, he could stand the mystery no longer and approached the stranger.

"Friend, may I ask who you are?"

The man looked at Gregory squarely and replied, "I am the poor merchant to whom you gave twelve pieces of money and the silver dish that held the special memory of your mother. I am your angel, whom God sent to test your charity."

Gregory began to tremble. An angel of God was before him!

"Fear not, Gregory. It is because of that silver dish that God has given you the Chair of Peter. As I was the cause of your being raised to that position, so shall I protect and preserve you in it until death. God will grant you everything you ask through me."

Then the angel vanished. Whether the other guests had even seen him, Gregory was not sure. But he was certain of the angel's words, for they still echoed in his head. And at the same time, he felt a remarkable sense of relief, as if the crushing weight of his responsibilities had been lifted.

Buoyed by his angel's promise, Gregory went on to accomplish more in a fourteen-year papacy than many kingdoms achieved in a generation. One of his greatest successes was the evangelization of England, which he accomplished through the missionary work of St. Augustine and monks from his own St. Andrew's Monastery.

When he died at age 64, Gregory left behind over 800 letters and numerous other writings. His influence on Christian civilization, and European history in general, was so profound as to earn him the titles "The Great" and "Doctor of the Church." Yet Gregory, in characteristic humility, always referred to himself as "the servant of the servants of God," a title that has been used ever since by the Popes.

Angels are pure spirits, neither male nor female, and therefore have no material bodies of their own. When angels appear on earth they assume human form for our benefit, so as not to overwhelm us with their beauty.

ST. ISIDORE AND THE PHANTOM FARMHAND

"Senor de Vergas, you must dismiss Isidore at once!" The angry foreman struck his sombrero against his leg, scattering dust in every direction.

"And what is the problem this time?" asked Juan de Vergas wearily.

"He is late for work every morning. And he talks out loud to no one! The other workers are upset. With the harvest upon us, Senor, we can't allow one man to cause such a disruption!"

Juan de Vergas listened carefully to his foreman's complaint. This wasn't the first time he had heard stories about his gentle laborer. It was rumored that Isidore spent his holidays with the poor in Madrid, sharing his meager food and belongings with them. And his frequent, vocal praying had been heard by all who had worked with him. Yet despite Isidore's odd reputation, his work was always done to satisfaction, often above and beyond. But now Juan de Vergas faced a more serious situation. If Isidore's behavior was affecting the other workers, something needed to be done.

"I will take care of it, Miguel," he said.

* * *

The next morning Juan de Vergas arose from bed at 4:00 a.m. and walked across his great estate to Isidore's small shack, where he hid himself behind a tree. It wasn't long before Isidore came out, walking quickly through the darkness, past his employer, and down the dirt road leading to the neighboring village.

After following Isidore for a mile, Juan de Vergas spotted the steeple of the village church and watched as Isidore entered. He decided to wait. Mass wouldn't last that long. As he waited, he felt a creeping distaste grow in his mouth for what he was doing. He genuinely liked Isidore and his wife, Mary. They worked hard without complaining. They were generous to a fault, though they themselves had very little. And yet here he was, trying to catch them in some vague, rumored wrongdoing.

The farm owner frowned. He recalled that sad day a few years back when Isidore and Mary's baby boy died. The whole estate had grieved with them. Yet the young couple had not shown a trace of self-pity and they were soon back to work. If anything, the ordeal seemed to strengthen their faith. Juan de Vergas wasn't so sure his own faith, weak as it was, would have survived such a tragedy.

After about forty minutes, a handful of villagers filed out of the small church. Juan de Vergas looked earnestly for his humble farmer among the passing faces, but nowhere did he see Isidore. Quietly he peered inside the church. There, kneeling before the altar, hands clasped tightly together, was Isidore. *This man's only crime is his passion for God*, thought Juan de Vergas. *The world could use more such criminals!*

Then, though he could see no one else in the dimly lit sanctuary except for Isidore, Juan de Vergas could have sworn he heard voices singing—beautiful voices with a lilt he had never heard before, not even in the majestic Cathedral of Madrid. He listened for several moments, unable to move as if caught in the spell of some wonderful enchantment. At last the singing stopped and a reverent silence fell back upon the church. Slightly perplexed, yet unexplainably happy,

Juan de Vergas returned to the estate house, leaving Isidore to pray.

* * *

The next morning, he followed Isidore to the church again. Once more Isidore remained behind long after Mass had ended. Though he heard no singing this time, Juan de Vergas could not bear to disturb his farmer. Obviously this ritual was important to Isidore; taking it away, he reasoned, would only bring more pain to a life that was embittered enough. Juan de Vergas decided instead to go to the fields. Perhaps he could explain Isidore's zeal to the others and convince them to be patient with their co-worker. He sought out Miguel.

"The workers are very happy, Senor," reported the foreman. "Whatever you said to Isidore seems to be working. He has been the first one in the fields, and has more than doubled his plowing the last two mornings."

Juan de Vergas stared at his foreman in disbelief. How could what he said be true?

Determined to find an answer, the following morning he followed Isidore to the small church again. The crisp autumn air reminded him that winter would soon be upon them. *I should take early morning walks more frequently*, he thought, as he went along the wooded path and listened joyfully to the praising sounds of the birds. It made him recall a story he had heard last winter . . .

Isidore and a companion had been walking along a similar forest trail on their way to the flour mill. They came upon some birds, neither chirping nor moving much, evidently weakened by the harsh winter and a lack of food. Upon seeing the poor birds, Isidore opened his corn sack and poured out half on the ground. The birds were delighted, but Isidore's companion was incensed. "The master will be furious!" he declared. (At this thought, Juan de Vergas chuckled. *Furious with Isidore? Not likely, even had he thrown down the whole bag!*)

The two men continued on to the mill. When they arrived, not only was Isidore's bag still full of corn, but after it was ground it produced twice as much flour as the other worker's full bag!

Yes, God looked after His beloved Isidore, of this Juan de Vergas had no doubt. To have such faith. What a gift! He wondered further what part, if any, God was playing in this new mystery.

This time after he watched Isidore enter the church, Juan de Vergas did not wait for Mass to end. Instead, he raced to the fields as soon as Isidore disappeared inside. He arrived at the edge of the hazy fields sweating, despite the morning chill. His breath was labored as he scanned the land before him.

Only one worker was out plowing at that early hour.

Surely that cannot be Isidore, thought Juan de Vergas. *Yet those are his oxen.*

He approached the lone figure in the field, making his way carefully through the early morning mist. Suddenly the fog cleared, and he stopped abruptly. For in front of him passed a strikingly handsome young man dressed all in white, with hair more golden than the surrounding wheat, and a face more radiant than the sun's reflection. As he guided the oxen past the startled farm owner, the young man's feet seemed to float over the ground. Despite the extraordinary sight before him, Juan de Vergas was not afraid. Peace and joy filled his soul in a way he had never before experienced.

He lost track of time as he watched and marveled at the wondrous vision in the field. Then slowly he became aware of other workers taking their posts. He looked around at their expressions, but no one seemed to acknowledge anything out of the ordinary. How could they not see? He turned back, but the luminous young man was gone.

Isidore became even more cherished to Juan de Vergas after that unforgettable morning and remained on the estate as a loyal worker for the rest of his life. He continued to talk to his guardian angel while working in the fields and led many of the other workers to lives of virtue through his Christian example. Isidore performed many miracles for the de Vergas family. His greatest accomplishment, however, was obtaining the gift of faith for his employer.

Isidore died a holy death on May 15, 1130. His wife, Mary, died a few years later and, like her husband, was later canonized a saint.

There are nine groups, or "choirs," of angels. The highest choir, the Seraphim, is believed to be nearest the Throne of God, loving, praising and glorifying Him ceaselessly. After the Seraphim follow the other eight choirs: Cherubim, Thrones, Dominations, Virtues, Powers, Principalities, Archangels, and Angels.

The Tradition of the Church teaches that Guardian Angels are taken from the Angel choir, and, in certain cases, the Archangel choir. These angels are at the lower end of the ranking not because they love God any less, but because they are in more direct contact with human beings and other visible works of creation.

They've even been known, on occasion, to do a little farmwork!

ST. MARGARET AND THE MESSENGER OF LOVE

"God hates me," spat the old man. "If there is a God at all."

Margaret was not surprised at the man's bitterness. She had seen many others like him, poor and unloved, who had lost all hope as they lay dying in the makeshift infirmary the Franciscans operated in Cortona's poor section. She gently repositioned the pillow under his head.

"There is a God," said Margaret firmly. "And He loves you dearly." She gave his bony hand a gentle squeeze. "Love him back! Unite your pain with the pain He felt on the Cross."

The old man didn't answer. But Margaret thought she detected a slight change, a bit of understanding perhaps, in his eyes. She could only hope that God would touch his heart before he died. Death, she knew, would come very soon for the old beggar.

Her duties done for the day, Margaret returned to her humble cottage, exhausted. The stench of sickness and sweat still lingered on her skin, but she was too tired to care. Her muscles ached with an intensity that should have made her yell out in pain, but she was silent. Physical conditions mattered little to Margaret. Her real agony was centered in her soul.

For many months now she had been preaching the message of God's love, and she was confident that she had reached at least a few souls. But despite the conversions she had witnessed firsthand, despite the arduous penances she forced upon herself, despite her sound words and devout actions, she could not bring herself to believe that God loved her.

She fell in a crumpled heap on the floor of her little shack, drawn toward the edge of despair. Like she had on so many other nights, Margaret began sobbing as feelings of self-loathing and sorrow filled her heart. She cried out in agony: "O Lord, can You ever love me again, as great as my sins have been?"

As convulsing sobs racked her bruised and tired body, Margaret wondered if she would ever be able to forget those events in her life that had led her to this wretched state . . .

* * *

Margaret had had a happy childhood in the Italian town of Laviano until, at the age of seven, she lost her mother whom she loved dearly. Her father remarried two years later, but young Margaret could draw no affection from her stern new stepmother.

As a young woman, Margaret was quite aware of her beauty, and couldn't help but be pleased when her fine features and spirited personality caught the attention of a handsome young nobleman from neighboring Montepulciano. Margaret instantly fell in love with him and was overjoyed at his suggestion they elope.

She went off with the young man and lived with him in his castle for nine years, but the promised marriage never took place. During this time they had a son together, adding to the scandal that already surrounded the couple. Margaret was an easy target for the townspeople's scorn, as she frequently rode through town fancily dressed and with a devil-may-care attitude.

But what the townspeople saw was only a part of Margaret, the part that enjoyed her luxurious surroundings and her companion's affection. Another part of her was deeply troubled by the sinful state she knew she had allowed her soul to fall into. Nonetheless, she was careful to keep her suffering conscience well hidden while she continued to assume an air of carefreeness around the castle and in town.

One day during Margaret's twenty-seventh year, her young nobleman went off on a journey. Several days later, when he was due to return, his dog came back alone and found Margaret. She became alarmed when the dog began tugging at her dress in frenzied distress. Margaret allowed the dog to lead her through the woods to a large oak tree. There she found the mutilated body of the nobleman thrown haphazardly into a pit at the base of the tree . . .

* * *

The recollection of finding her companion's body under that tree made Margaret gasp aloud. Startled, she sat up and surveyed her dingy surroundings. She was alone. There was no dog, no tree, no body — all were now just a memory. But the sorrow and guilt she had felt upon making her grisly discovery made her tremble now as before.

"O Jesus, that could have been me, my body ravaged by worms while my soul . . ." She could not bear to finish the thought. She often wondered if she was in some way responsible for her lover's death. Perhaps she had unwittingly stirred a rivalry between him and another man, or unknowingly offended an enemy during a trip to town.

But it was the possibility of his soul being condemned that most cruelly tore at Margaret's heart. What if she was to blame? Could she have saved him somehow from that terrible end?

Suddenly Margaret was aware of a brilliant light breaking the darkness in which she sat. She looked up in surprise, then gasped in disbelief. Standing before her was a person more splendid, more beautiful than she would have thought possible. Rays of light seemed to pour forth from every inch of his white-robed body. His face, while princely, emanated kindness. But it was his eyes that captured

Margaret's attention the most. They were filled with love—a pure, unconditional love that was directed right at her.

"Have no fear, Margaret," said the vision. "I am your guardian angel."

Margaret's heart skipped a beat, so overwhelmed with joy and awe was she at that moment. The angel's voice was familiar, as if she had heard it whispering in her head on past occasions.

"Margaret," said the angel tenderly. "Be assured God loves you more than you could ever conceive."

Like water breaking forth from behind a dam, a peace unlike Margaret had ever known flooded her soul. *Oh, was it really true? How could it not be, coming from this heavenly messenger?*

"You need not prove your sincerity to the Lord," continued the angel. "He knows what is in your heart. He has forgiven you."

To Margaret's great delight, her angel remained with her for a long time that night. He answered her questions, resolved her doubts, and quieted her distress. He reassured her that her penances and good works were pleasing to the Lord.

If only I had known such peace existed! thought Margaret. As she basked in the comforting glow of her angel's presence, she recalled the first steps she had made along her journey back to God . . .

* * *

After the death of her companion, Margaret immediately resolved to repent. She gave away all of her possessions and traveled to Cortona with her young son. The Friars Minor of Cortona were renowned far and wide for their kindness to everyone. Margaret thought that perhaps they would take pity on her. Her hopes were realized when the friars, moved by Margaret's sincerity and determination, agreed to direct her spiritual renewal.

During those first years with the Franciscans, Margaret battled temptations by imposing rigorous penances and acts of self-mortification upon herself. She slept on the hard ground, dressed in rags, and cut and bruised her beautiful face to make herself appear ugly. More than once the friars had to intercede and stop Margaret from these extreme practices, fearing that she would permanently harm herself.

* * *

As her thoughts came back to the present, Margaret felt a slight panic stir in her heart. With her angel still near, she sensed she was being told that all those physical tortures she had been putting herself through were not in themselves going to bring her closer to God. But what else did she possibly have to give?

Fear not, Margaret, a kindly voice echoed in her head. *I will show you.*

From that night on, Margaret's guardian angel appeared to her regularly and tutored her intensively in matters of advanced spirituality. She was an ardent student and soon reached the point where possessing God's love was not enough. She burned with the desire to give back to God a love so fierce and so strong that it would unite her completely with Him.

Margaret's spiritual transformation under the gentle coaching of her angel soon became apparent to the Franciscan fathers who had taken her in. Convinced of her desire for holiness, they allowed her to become a full member in the Third Order of St. Francis.

With burning zeal Margaret threw herself into corporal works of mercy, devoting herself in particular to the sick poor in Cortona. Soon her persuasive personality and inherent goodness attracted other women and men to work with her. With the support of some of these influential citizens, she eventually persuaded the city council to help her open a hospital to serve the needs of the poor.

Although many things had become clearer to Margaret through her experiences with the Franciscans and under the tutelage of her angel, there still remained a question in her mind: Why had God granted her so many consolations and favors? Her question was answered one night when her angel appeared to her again, but this time in the company of the Lord Himself.

Jesus said to her: "I have put you as a burning light, to enlighten those who sit in the darkness. . . Show how you are converted; call others to repentance. The graces I have bestowed on you are not meant for you alone."

Margaret wasted no time in acting upon the Lord's words. She began a campaign against sin and vice the like of which had never been seen in Cortona. Soon large numbers of people, ranging from the mildly curious to the horribly wicked, flocked to Cortona to hear her words and to witness for themselves the miracles of healing and conversion that surrounded Margaret. Her reputation spread as far as France and Spain, and not without effect. Soon hundreds were doing penance, settling disputes, and returning to the Church.

Margaret's last years were very difficult, for even in light of all the good she had done, there were still those who doubted her sincerity, as well as her sanity. Some hardened residents of Cortona even went so far as to accuse her of sinful relationships with the friars. Her angel became ever more dear to her during these times, comforting her in her loneliness and soothing the physical pains that she continued to impose upon herself as atonement for the sins of her youth.

In 1297, at the age of fifty, as she received the Anointing of the Sick from the friar who had taken her in twenty-nine years ago, Margaret recalled the angel's words from one of their lessons together: "The highest degree of love is a desire which inflames the spirit like fire. In this final state the soul never ceases to seek her beloved, her spouse everywhere and in everything."

Margaret truly believed she was now ready to unite with her Beloved, the One she had been seeking all these years. Suddenly her angel was at her side. *Dear friend!* She reached out her hand to meet his. His final, reassuring words to her as they left this world together echoed his first many years ago: "God loves you more than you could ever conceive."

Our angels never give up on us, even when we fall into serious sin. On the contrary, they work that much harder to get us to repent. They stir in our consciences feelings of sorrow and guilt. They lead us toward the Sacrament of Penance and help us make good confessions by reminding us of our sins.

The angels' greatest desire is for us to share their holiness in heaven, and to that end they work unceasingly, no matter what we've done. It is no wonder then that Jesus reminds us in Scripture: "I tell you, there is joy before the angels of God over one sinner who repents."

ST. LYDWINE AND THE CELESTIAL NAVIGATOR

"Come on, Lydwine! You'll soon be skating by yourself at that speed!"

Oh no, I won't. Just watch me!

Pursing her lips and clenching her jaw, the attractive sixteen-year-old Dutch girl gave a mighty push with her right leg. She sailed across the ice with the ease of a knife slicing through butter.

In spite of the cold wind slapping at her face, Lydwine couldn't remember the last time she was this happy. To think the doctors had told her just last month she wouldn't skate again! Of course, she could understand their dire prediction; after all, she had been confined to bed for weeks with a mysterious ailment that had left her unable to move her legs at all, to say nothing about skating on them.

But as mysteriously as the disease had struck, it had just as mysteriously retreated. And not a day too soon, as far as Lydwine was concerned. The good skating weather was almost over.

Her friends were now easily within reach. "Lydwine!" someone shouted. "Lydwine!"

Yes, yes, she thought, *I am almost upon you. Surprised, eh?*

"Lydwine, look out!"

The sudden force that hit her from behind and lifted her into the air was mild compared to the force of the ice breaking her fall. Panic seized her as she gasped for air and found none. She saw the worried looks, heard the urgent voices.

"I didn't see her . . . so sorry!"

"Is she all right?"

"Get the doctor!

Then the faces and the voices and the pain faded from Lydwine's perception as she slipped off, gratefully, into unconsciousness.

* * *

"Papa, what's wrong with me?" cried Lydwine. It had been more than three months since the skating accident. Not only had her broken rib failed to heal, but she had gotten sicker by the day. The doctors told her a tumor had formed under the broken rib and had burst.

But that seemed to be all the doctors knew. One of them had just finished examining her, the same quizzical look crossing his face that Lydwine had seen dozens of times before in the past weeks. *Why can't they do something?* She wanted to scream but could manage only a moan.

Just then another wave of nausea hit her. She turned her head, the only part of her body she could move, and vomited. The bitter taste in her mouth matched the bitter tears that streamed down her face. *Oh, Papa, what is wrong with me? Please, Papa, please help me!*

But no answers were destined to come any time soon. For four years Lydwine continued to suffer the most torturous maladies to the complete bafflement of her family and doctors. She was unable to sit or stand. Only by lying on her stomach with her legs drawn up underneath her chest could she bear the terrible pain that invaded every part of her body. Severe headaches, toothaches, fever, and thirst besieged her day and night. Unexplained hemorrhaging occurred from her mouth, nose, and ears.

Only one person could bring Lydwine any consolation during those days and nights of agony: Father John Pot. At first, Lydwine resisted her parish priest's attempts to comfort her. Why should she listen to this man of God when God had turned a deaf ear to her? She had assaulted heaven with her pleas and prayers, but it seemed to Lydwine that God had all but abandoned her when she needed Him most.

Father Pot, however, knew otherwise. He persistently counseled Lydwine and prayed over her, and gradually his efforts paid off.

"Father, I understand now!" Lydwine exclaimed jubilantly one day. "God is not punishing me. He is asking for my help to save souls."

Father Pot smiled. He thanked God for sending to Lydwine the grace to accept her suffering. While many would have judged Lydwine's new-found fervor a symptom of delirium, Father Pot was confident that her change of heart was genuine. He saw no madness in her eyes when she spoke, but only the clearest joy and love.

"What good I can do, Father. I want to help so many souls! O please, dear God, let me not waste my sufferings any longer!"

* * *

Life was drastically different for Lydwine from that point on. Her physical sufferings remained; in fact, they came to her in greater intensity. But her mental anguish was gone. Far from thinking that God had abandoned her, she knew now without a doubt that He was near. Jesus often appeared to her in visions as she lay helpless in her room. The Blessed Virgin also visited her and comforted her in motherly fashion.

But Lydwine's most frequent consolation came from the loving ministry of her guardian angel, who was nearly always visible to her now. On a few occasions he lit up her room so brightly that neighbors feared a fire had broken out!

"It is just my angel," Lydwine would tell the worried neighbors. Of course, when they looked around the room, they saw nothing.

Lydwine's angel was not just a bedside companion, however. He knew how deeply the soul in his charge missed being able to walk and run, to skate and frolic. And so he provided her with a wonderful alternative.

"Lydwine, let us go on a journey together," he said one night to the bewildered girl.

"How can I go anywhere when I'm confined to this bed?"

"I will show you."

As the angel took her hand, Lydwine felt her soul rising out of her body. How was this possible? Was she dead?

You are very much alive, she heard her angel answer her inside her head. *Come see the wonders of God's universe!*

Suddenly Lydwine found herself in a strange new place. And yet she had not even blinked!

The land before her was dry and harsh looking. The sun was low in the western sky, throwing long shadows off the rocky hillsides. Lydwine was atop one of the hills, the tallest on the landscape. A crowd of olive-skinned men and women was gathered nearby. Though Lydwine and her angel were quite close to them, as near as Lydwine could tell in her bodiless form, no one seemed aware of them. The crowd was reverently silent, as if the very air held great mysteries to be contemplated.

"Behold, Lydwine," spoke her angel, "the place where Jesus Christ died for all."

Golgotha! Lydwine had sensed they were in a holy place. Her instincts had been right. The angel handed her a sliver of dark brown wood.

"Take this piece of the True Cross. It has been buried here, undiscovered for all these years. Jesus wishes for you to have it, so perfectly have you united your sufferings with His."

Lydwine clutched the wood tightly and closed her eyes. When she opened them again, she was back in her room. In her bed.

"Well, our Lydwine has returned to us!" The relieved voice of her kindly nurse echoed in Lydwine's ears. She blinked at the woman, wide-eyed.

"You mean you saw me leave and come back?" Lydwine asked.

"In a manner of speaking, dear. One minute you were saying your Hail Mary's, and the next you were quiet and still, frozen up like the canal in winter. I thought you had finally gone to sweet Jesus and the angels for sure!"

Lydwine was disappointed. She had been with Jesus and the angels, but, evidently, only in a dream. She hadn't actually "gone" anywhere. Then she remembered something. She opened her right hand slowly and peeked down. It was there! The piece of the Cross!

A light caught her eye and she looked up. In the corner of her room stood her angel, smiling at her affectionately.

Thank you, dear friend, thought Lydwine. *If I live to be a thousand, I shall never forget this night.*

We have many more places to visit, answered the angel. *Wait and see!*

True to his word, the angel took Lydwine on many other spiritual pilgrimages. On each occasion, her body entered a trance-like state, while her spirit soared with her angel guide. They explored famous shrines, holy lands, and faraway monasteries. They strolled the pathways of ancient Eden and chatted with the saints in the halls of heaven. And sometimes they went only as far as the nearby parish church to visit Jesus in the Blessed Sacrament.

It was purgatory, however, in which they spent the most time. Lydwine had always had a great devotion to the souls in purgatory and offered to God many of her own sufferings to speed their entrance into heaven. The trips she made to purgatory with her angel were difficult for Lydwine. She once confessed she could only endure going because her presence brought some comfort to the souls there.

"Dear angel, who is that?" she asked her guardian during one of their trips to a particularly grim section of purgatory. She had spotted a very sad-looking angel sitting on the rim of what appeared to be a well. Cries of agony echoed up from within its depths.

"That is the guardian of the soul you asked me about," her angel replied. Lydwine remembered that she had wondered about a man she helped convert and who had died of the plague twelve years before.

"He is still here? she asked incredulously. While Lydwine had never ceased praying for the man, she was somewhat surprised that he was still in purgatory.

"He died quickly after his confession, before he could do the penance necessary for his sins," explained the angel. "Would you be willing to endure some more pain in order to diminish his?"

"With all my heart," she quickly replied. At that very moment Lydwine felt her pains intensify. She was brought out of her ecstasy with a violent tremor.

"How frightful are the prisons of purgatory!" she cried out to the startled visitors in her room.

Several days later, Lydwine was rewarded for her courage and devotion. An angel appeared to her when she was alone one morning. It was not her own guardian, but she recognized the blessed spirit instantly as the angel who had been sitting on the edge of the well in purgatory. He came to proclaim good news, he told her. The soul under his care had been freed!

Long after the angel left her, Lydwine remained exultant. Her pain and tears were not going to waste! She thanked God for allowing her to see the difference she was making in people's lives.

Lydwine offered her sufferings for all souls, but those she had the most fervor for were the souls of priests. Her guardian angel helped her in this special mission by showing her the souls of bad priests and exposing their sinful thoughts and intentions. With great zeal, Lydwine prayed and sacrificed for their conversions.

As Lydwine increased in age and sanctity, so her sufferings increased in number and intensity. She lost the sight in her right eye. A cleft running from her forehead to her nose horribly disfigured her once beautiful face. Convulsions, vomiting, fever, and pain racked her body unceasingly. Her stomach burst open on one occasion and she had to be bound up tightly to keep from literally falling apart.

Yet asked once if she wished to be healed, Lydwine replied, "No, there is but one thing now that I desire; it is not to be deprived of my discomforts and pains."

Lydwine's reputation for holiness quickly became known far and wide. Pilgrims flocked by the hundreds to her tiny room where she remained, physically at least, a prisoner to her infirmities. The first thing these astonished visitors noticed was the smell of sweet perfume that came forth from her festering sores. Many were rewarded with other miracles. Healings, prophecies, conversions, and exorcisms left throngs of curious onlookers—believers and skeptics alike—shaking their heads.

During the last seven years of her life, Lydwine took no food or drink. She subsisted on Holy Communion alone. Her guardian angel, as well as many other angels, kept her constant company during this time. Their unearthly beauty gave her the greatest joy and consolation.

On Easter Tuesday 1433, Lydwine's sufferings finally came to an end. As she took her last breath, she felt the familiar release from her body that always preceded her spiritual wanderings. An incomparable joy filled her spirit. *Oh, dear angel, this is the moment, isn't it? The moment I've been waiting for all my life.* She looked down on the lifeless body below her—now miraculously free of all wounds, scars, and deformities—and hoped that the tortured existence she spent in it on earth had made her worthy for the glory of heaven.

You have done well, Lydwine. Come, the Lord is waiting. Then, once again, Lydwine's angel reached out and guided her soul through a different dimension to a faraway place.

This time for good.

The guardian angels are great sources of consolation for the holy souls in purgatory. According to early Church Fathers, the guardian angel leads the soul to purgatory and thereafter visits and consoles that soul until its release. The angel also helps the soul by inspiring friends and relatives left on earth to pray and offer Masses for their loved one.

ST. ROSE AND THE BELOVED COMPANION

Peacefully exhausted after an evening of prayer in her little hermitage, Rose walked through the garden of her parents' estate toward the large house she shared with her family. Meditations from the Rosary still lingered in her memory and brought a faint smile to her lips. She could have easily remained at the hermitage and prayed until dawn. But tonight she knew she must follow her mind, not her heart. And her mind told her to get some sleep. In the morning she would need her full strength to face the Court of the Inquisition.

When Rose had first heard the news that eminent theologians were on their way to Lima to question her, she was bewildered. What could they possibly want with her, a simple lay Dominican? She knew that some of the townspeople talked behind her back. At times, she supposed, she did get carried away with her prayers and penances. But if the Inquisitors were going to take her to task for loving God too much, then so be it!

Strengthened with new resolve, Rose strode confidently to the gate at the edge of the garden and gave it a push. It didn't budge. Mother must have forgotten to unlock it, Rose thought. She looked around for something to break the lock with, but the moonless night made her search futile. Rose sighed. She didn't want to wake the whole household by shouting for help. She decided she would go back to the hut. It wouldn't be the first time she had slept there.

Just then a light caught Rose's attention. Mother! She remembered and is coming to open the gate! But as the light swelled in brilliance, Rose realized it wasn't coming from her parents' window. It was coming from just inside the gate, behind a clump of bushes. Rose stood transfixed as the luminous orb danced its way toward her. Suddenly it stopped, and in the blink of an eye a striking young man appeared in its place.

Rose's heart leapt with delight, for she knew this visitor from many times before. How glad she was to see him now!

"Thank you, my dear angel," she whispered. As the gate swung open, Rose rushed inside to be near her friend.

"You will do fine tomorrow," the angel assured her, gazing tenderly into her eyes.

Rose smiled back. She knew she would sleep well now. And she knew that come morning, she had nothing to fear. Her guardian angel had told her so.

* * *

Isabel de Flores was born in Lima, Peru, on April 20, 1586. Little Isabel's Indian maid looked at the child one day and exclaimed, "Our beautiful baby looks just like a rose!" Never would the young woman have guessed just how many people in coming ages would invoke that nickname in tender reverence.

As a young child, Rose decided on a course of life symbolized, in part, by her name. But it wasn't the sweetness and softness of the rose petals that she embraced. Rather, it was the thorns. Three days a week she would allow herself only a small bit of bread and a cup of warm water. And as often as she could, she would run off to pray while the other children played merrily and wondered where their playmate went.

At an early age, under the tutelage of her patient and loving mother, Rose learned to read and write. Her quick mastery of the language was so remarkable that those who knew Rose felt she had been given Divine assistance. Rose herself didn't care how she had learned. She was simply overjoyed when she could finally read the life of her heroine, St. Catherine of Siena.

Many years later, at the age of twenty, Rose followed Catherine's example by joining the Third Order of St. Dominic, a secular order of religious men and women. Donning the same black and white Dominican habit that Catherine wore nearly three hundred years earlier, she called herself Rosa de Santa Maria.

While that day was one of the happiest for Rose, it was not so for her parents. They had been urging her to marry, hoping that a good husband would help the family financially. Although her parents were not poor by any means—her father was a member of the Spanish viceroy's guard—thirteen children took a toll on the family's resources.

Rose helped in whatever ways she could by selling needlework, flowers, and fruit at the market. But the trips into town were not always pleasant for Rose. Her outspoken love for her faith combined with severe, even bizarre, acts of self-mortification, such as rubbing pepper on her face to make herself ugly, had gained her an unwanted reputation. Taunts, jeers, and scornful laughter greeted Rose wherever she went.

"Here comes Saint Rose!"

"Heal me, O holy one!"

"Take her to the sea so she can walk on the water!"

Rose ignored the ridicule as best she could. She knew Jesus faced even greater humiliation on His way to Calvary. But why did they have to mock her best friend, too?

"Who's she talking to now?"

"Her guardian angel, of course! Don't you see the wings of gold?"

Rose always wondered about such remarks. Why was it so surprising that she should be talking to her angel? Didn't everyone? For as long as she could remember, her guardian angel was always at her side, very often as visible to her as one of her brothers or sisters. They sang together as she embroidered her silks. He delivered messages for her at all hours of the day and night. And he kept her company during the long hours she spent in prayer. In fact, Rose once stated that there was nothing her guardian angel would not do for her.

And at times, he did things she didn't want him to do. Her fasts and other penances often left her sick. On many of these occasions, her angel ignored her protests to be left alone and brought her whatever medicine she needed to recover — no matter the time of day or night.

As a means to intensify her spiritual life, Rose arranged for a small hut to be built in her parents' garden. When her work was done for the day, she couldn't walk fast enough to her little hermitage to pray and do penance. She often passed the night away there in prayer and contemplation, her guardian angel close to her side in the little five-by-four-foot enclosure.

As much as the reclusive life appealed to Rose, she knew she was called to do more. And so she set up an infirmary in her parents' house, where she took in poor Indian women, children, and slaves. She instructed them in the truths of the Faith and won numerous souls to Christ.

It wasn't long before Rose's ministry to the Indians, the conversions she gained, her reported visions and ecstasies, and her extreme penitential lifestyle all caught the attention of suspicious Church officials. Much to her dismay, Rose found herself called before the Inquisitors.

The morning of her questioning, Rose sat peacefully before her examiners. She met their eyes and answered their questions without hesitation. And when they were done, the Grand Inquisitors of the Royal Court of Imperial Spain, eminent theologians all, came to a startling conclusion: Rosa de Santa Maria not only possessed genuine holiness, but also a level of theological knowledge that had to have been Divinely given her.

Her angel had been right. She had done just fine.

That evening, after the Inquisitors had departed on their journey back to Spain, Rose hurried to her little retreat in the garden. She didn't want to be late. For some time now Jesus had been appearing to her daily in the form of the Holy Infant. On one of His visits He had lovingly called her "Rose of my Heart." She had almost died of joy! She quickened her pace a little, for she had so much to confide to Jesus. She must see Him tonight!

But as the hour of the Lord's expected calling came and went, Rose began to fret. Had she done something to offend Him? she wondered. He must come tonight. He must!

"Dear angel, you must help me!" implored Rose. Her heart nearly broken, she began to sing.

A citizen passing by noticed a very bright light coming from the Flores family garden. A melancholic, but hauntingly rhythmic, chant sailed over the still night air:

> Fly, O Swift Messenger,
> Fly to Our Lord!
> Oh, hasten to our Master adored!
> Ask why he delays and remains
> Far from our side.
>
> Fly, Noble Messenger, fly!
> Tell Him when He is not here
> I languish alone.
> Tell Him His Rose must her sorrow bemoan
> Till the moment when He shall return!

The citizen stopped to listen, mesmerized by the mysterious light and the hypnotic chant. Then suddenly, a movement. No! It couldn't be! He blinked. Looked again. Nothing. A trick of the light, he decided. The weary traveler continued toward home, a strange yet comforting melody still ringing in his ears.

And a faint image of a child floating in the air tickling his imagination.

Just as no two people are alike, no two angels are alike. St. Thomas goes so far as to say that each angel is an entirely different species unto itself. Each angel is distinct in the way it reflects God's goodness, beauty, and power.

Moreover, each guardian angel has been matched perfectly, as only God could do, to its human companion. Our angels have complete knowledge of us and, accordingly, know what is best for us, even when we might beg to differ.

ST. FRANCES OF ROME AND THE HEAVENLY HELPERS

Frances wrung out a fresh cloth with her right hand while grasping her son's fingers with her left. She carefully wiped the perspiration from his feverish forehead and did her best to look cheerful and confident.

"There, Evangelista, a cool cloth and a little soup and you'll be back playing in no time," Frances assured him. But the words sounded hollow to her. She knew Evangelista would not survive the deadly plague that had struck Rome and the surrounding region.

If only the boy could see his father one last time, she thought. A nobleman, Lorenzo Ponziano had been taken prisoner by the opposing faction in a civil war. Their other son, Battista, was also being held as a hostage to vanquish the Ponziano family's resistance in the war.

The temptation to give up gnawed at her like it had many times before. But so many still depended on her. The sick, the starving. But most of all, now, her son. She looked down tenderly on his innocent face. He had always been a good boy. Even now on his deathbed he talked in what little voice he had of the goodness of God.

Suddenly a change came over Evangelista. He gazed up into the air, a look of wonderment crossed his face, and for the first time in days his fever-ridden body stopped trembling. After several moments in this private ecstasy, he turned to Frances and smiled. "The angels have come to take me to heaven! Mother, I will remember you!"

Frances fought to choke back her sobs. "And I you, my dear son. Now, go with them. Go to God." Through her tears Frances looked upon the peaceful face of Evangelista and knew that angels had indeed taken him to Paradise. How comforting were his last words to her! And yet how she missed him so already.

Though her heart ached, Frances knew that God had not abandoned her. What she didn't know was that in a year's time He would grant her an extraordinary favor for her love and trust.

And Evangelista would be at his mother's side to witness it.

* * *

Frances' life had not always been so difficult. In marked contrast to her later years, she was born into a wealthy Roman family and raised in the lap of luxury.

But the rich life held no appeal for the pious young Frances, and at age eleven she declared to her parents her desire to become a nun.

Her parents flatly refused. Though they cared for her deeply, they would not watch her throw her birthright away. And so a little more than a year later, they arranged for her to marry Lorenzo Ponziano, a handsome young nobleman. Frances was heartbroken but silenced her objections in a spirit of obedience.

Frances had just turned thirteen when she and Lorenzo were wed. Her husband was a good man who loved her very much. He gave her all the fineries a young girl could ever want and treated her tenderly and respectfully. But before long the entertaining and socializing that were expected of a nobleman's wife took an ill effect on Frances. She collapsed one day and remained bedridden for months, unable at times to even eat or speak.

One day during her affliction, she had a vision of St. Alexis, a nobleman who had run off to become a beggar rather than be married. He asked Frances if she wanted to recover, or if she was prepared to die. "God's will is mine," she answered.

"Then you will live to glorify His Name," declared the saint. He then covered her with his cloak and disappeared. Afterward, Frances made an immediate and complete recovery to the amazement of family and friends.

Her health restored, Frances devoted herself to doing God's work in every way she could while still fulfilling her secular duties. She spent many hours praying, visiting hospitals, and distributing alms. But she quickly put everything else aside when she was needed by her husband and children. Frances once said that a married woman must at times leave God at the altar to find Him in her housekeeping.

Life presented new challenges beginning in 1408 when a hostile political faction took over Rome. Citizens were murdered, farms were burned, and houses were plundered, including the Ponziano's. Just when it looked like it could get no worse, plague descended upon the land and claimed the life of little Evangelista.

Though trials of such magnitude would have driven many to despair, Frances refused to give in to that temptation. In the year following her son's death, Frances worked feverishly to turn what remained of her house into a hospital and shelter for the homeless. She recruited the help of other women, many of whom gave up their wealth and high positions in society to answer Frances' call. Frances embodied the very essence of heroic virtue, and God did not let it go unnoticed.

While praying in the chapel on the one-year anniversary of Evangelista's death, Frances found herself filled with an unexpected happiness. Suddenly, from out of nowhere, a brilliant light filled the room, forcing Frances to close her eyes. When she opened them a moment later, she gasped in disbelief.

In the middle of the radiance stood Evangelista. Frances gazed upon her son with a mixture of love and awe. For while he looked the same as she remembered, right down to the clothes he had last worn, he had been transfigured to a point of breathtaking beauty and perfection.

By Evangelista's side was another boy whose features were even more splendid. Though Frances was acutely aware of this other boy's beauty, she nevertheless turned her full attention on her son. She reached out to embrace him but found she could not grasp his ethereal body.

Evangelista greeted his mother and consoled her. He told her how happy he was in heaven and how the angels were his constant companions. Then he introduced the being at his side. "My companion is an archangel. In heaven he occupies a place above mine. God sends him to you, dear mother, to be of comfort to you in this life. He will not leave you night or day, and you shall have the sweet satisfaction of seeing him constantly with your bodily eyes."

Evangelista remained with Frances for an hour before he returned to heaven. After watching her son fade from her vision, Frances timidly looked over to where the glorious archangel still stood. She thanked God for sending such a wonderful gift. While she wanted nothing more than to be with God and Evangelista in Paradise, she realized she had work yet to do on earth. And now she had a heavenly helper at her side to see her through her labors.

As Evangelista promised, the archangel remained with Frances every moment for the next twenty-three years of her life. He gave off such a brilliant light that Frances could not look directly at him without hurting her eyes. On certain occasions, such as when she was in prayer or talking to her confessor, the angel's light would dim, allowing her to see his features clearly. He always appeared as a boy of about nine years old. His beautiful golden hair flowed over his shoulders. And he wore at differing times a white, red or blue tunic over a long shining robe.

Frances had long been troubled by vicious attacks from Satan, who hated the love for God she carried in her heart. Sometimes these attacks were in the forms of particularly troubling temptations. At other times they took on the forms of hideous apparitions. But when she was most frightened, her angel would merely shake his hair — the source, it seemed, of his brilliant light — and the evil spirit would flee.

At other times the light from the angel allowed Frances to see the secret thoughts and sins carried in the minds and hearts of people she encountered. Frances brought many souls back to God by means of this special gift.

True to Evangelista's words, the archangel was nearly always visible to Frances. Only when she committed a fault, even the slightest, did the angel fade from her view. But he always returned as soon as she made a sincere confession. Frances learned to value these admonishments from her companion, for they helped her master the virtue of humility.

Frances valued the guidance of her angel in other areas of life as well, particularly the day-to-day responsibilities she found so boring.

"How can these menial household tasks be furthering my spiritual progress?" she cried out in frustration one day. "Are they not just wasted hours?"

"Frances," replied the angel. "God's will is to be found in all tasks, big or small, and on all occasions, of major or minor importance."

In addition to spiritual help, the angel also assisted Frances in more temporal ways. His brilliant light, for instance, allowed her to read and move about the house late at night without a candle. And once, when her acts of self-mortification were too severe, he gently delivered this reminder: "God never intended that the spirit should ruin the flesh and return it to him despoiled."

In 1414, to Frances' great joy, Lorenzo was allowed to come home after four years of exile. Back in Rome he saw for himself the degree of sanctity his wife had attained. Others had heard about her reputation as well, and came from all over the region seeking cures, conversions, and other miracles through her intercession.

Lorenzo soon realized that he could not keep his wife for himself. He agreed to free her from her domestic duties (she would still, however, remain his wife) so that she could devote herself to achieving a long-desired goal: forming a religious order.

Ever since Frances had encouraged other Roman women to help her with the sick and the poor, she had hoped to someday form them into a religious community. Now her dream could become a reality. With Lorenzo's support and the help of her confessor, Frances founded the Oblates of Mary. The members took no vows. They remained laywomen who made simple pledges to offer themselves to God and serve the poor.

Frances worked tirelessly with the Oblates. Daily she relied upon the strength of her heavenly companion to help her manage the myriad of duties that confronted her. On one occasion the archangel even intervened in the life of another Oblate, when he prevented the despairing woman from committing suicide.

After Lorenzo's death, Frances decided it was time to join the order she had founded. On that day in 1436 when she formally entered the community, she received a vision of Jesus seated on a glorious throne and surrounded by countless angels. Then the Lord chose an angel from the Choir of Powers and assigned him to take the place of the archangel as Frances' special guardian for the remaining years of her life.

When the vision ended, Frances turned her head, not quite sure what to expect. Had she been dreaming?

No! The angel in the vision was right there beside her. He was even more beautiful and radiant than her archangel, and in his left hand he carried three golden palm branches. They symbolized, he later told her, the virtues of charity, prudence, and firmness—virtues which would mark Frances' mission with the Oblates.

This angel became as dear to Frances in the last years of her life as the archangel had been during her middle years. He helped her carry out her duties as Superior of the Oblates while using every opportunity to prepare Frances for her own death, which, he reminded her constantly, was imminent.

Four years later, on March 9, 1440, the angel's prediction came true. As Frances lay on her deathbed, she thought back to the torturous days and nights she nursed her son and husband as they lay dying. Finally the day had come when she would be reunited with them!

Oh death, where is your sting? thought Frances. *I feel nothing but love! So much love surrounds me!*

Near at her side was her beautiful spirit friend. And next to him stood the archangel who had been her companion for so many years. On her other side was yet another angel whom she was seeing for the first time, yet she knew him to be her guardian from birth.

They were all there to lead her home.

The blessed Power bent down and whispered in her ear. And then Frances spoke her last words:

"The angel has finished his task; he beckons me to follow him."

St. Thomas taught that God appoints additional angels to persons with the responsibility of leading others, particularly in spiritual matters. Often, as in the case of St. Frances, these extra helpers are taken from a higher choir of angels. Just think how many angels the Pope must have at his side!

ST. JOHN BOSCO AND THE BIG GRAY DOG

"If only my Grigio were here," John Bosco muttered under his breath. He hoped the young priest at his side didn't hear the apprehension in his voice. There was no need to upset him any further.

For hours the two priests had been on the road to Ventimiglia, a town on the French-Italian border. When they had started the journey, the weather had been fine. But a storm had caught them by surprise and slowed their pace. Now they wouldn't make it to town before nightfall.

He prayed silently that they wouldn't become lost in the stormy darkness, or fall prey to roving robbers who stalked the roadways.

In his younger days, Don ("Father") Bosco would have thought little of such challenges. But now, at age 73, he was not so eager to walk along the path of danger. More importantly, there was the safety of his young companion to worry about.

"Who is Grigio, Father?" asked the younger priest.

Don Bosco sighed. "Ah, who is Grigio, you ask. That's a good question, my son. A good question."

The old priest's mind went back in time. Oblivious to the rain driving into his face, he thought back to that night in 1854, more than thirty years ago, when he first met Il Grigio . . .

* * *

The night was just as dark. Though no storm hindered Don Bosco's journey, the surroundings were every bit as threatening. He had heard rumors that assassination attempts were being planned on his life. But he couldn't very well just hide in his rectory. There was so much work to be done! His parishioners needed him. His boys needed him!

And so, as many times in the past, he found himself on the seedy streets of Turin, making his way back to the rectory after a late-night sick call. While he had no intention of cutting back on his ministerial duties, he did make a mental note to be a bit more cautious. The next time he was called to a rough section of the Italian city, he would bring a couple of his larger students along with him.

He smiled when he pictured Marcus and Angelo lumbering alongside him. He knew they would jump at the thought of helping their padre.

He suddenly sensed a presence behind him. Nervously he looked back. A large dark-colored dog was following him. He had not thought about this sort of trouble!

But there was something about this dog that quickly put Don Bosco at ease, and soon the furry intruder was walking alongside the priest. The more unsavory-looking characters he passed on the streets, the more Don Bosco became very thankful that the dog was with him. When they reached the rectory, the dog eagerly accepted Don Bosco's pat on the head. Then he turned around and padded silently off into the night.

Time to find your own way home now, friend, thought the priest.

Hanging up his coat and hat inside the warm confines of the rectory, Don Bosco considered it fortuitous indeed that the dog had appeared out of nowhere to accompany him home. For although he normally didn't put much stock in the endless talk behind his back, these latest murmurings of an attempt on his life made him more than a little apprehensive.

He knew that many people were upset with him. Political and religious groups alike had made no secret of their dislike for the active priest. Local political leaders claimed he was harboring young criminals. Don Bosco believed that the politicians were simply jealous of his remarkable fundraising abilities—especially when none of the money went their way! Certain religious organizations, particularly the Waldensians—a splintered Catholic sect—disliked him for his orthodox preaching and his loyalty to the Pope.

Don Bosco chuckled to himself. *How many there are who would like to get their hands around my neck! But they're going to have to work for the chance!*

If his enemies worked hard to stop him, Don Bosco worked even harder to frustrate them. "God will help us," was the priest's frequent battle cry, and it seemed to many that only with the help of God could he have accomplished all that he did.

From an early age, Don Bosco felt drawn to a vocation of working with young boys. After his ordination in 1841, he began his work in earnest, seeking out the homeless and troubled youths in the ghettos and the jails. He housed them, fed them, and taught them about God's love for them. He devoted Sundays in particular to the boys, combining Mass and catechism lessons with magic shows and juggling acts.

His most recent success had been the opening of a vocational workshop for the boys, where they trained to be tailors, shoemakers, carpenters, and bookkeepers. Financing the workshops had not been easy. Don Bosco worked hard to gain the support, financial and otherwise, of the local citizens, who at first were suspicious of the priest's "band of ruffians." But it wasn't long before they realized that the priest was actually deterring the boys from a life in crime. Soon there were enough donations to build a church for Don Bosco's growing flock.

But there still remained much to be done. And Don Bosco would not be scared away by either political or religious extremists.

Despite his best intentions to be more cautious, Don Bosco was soon out traveling alone again on the city streets. Alone, that is, in terms of other people. For strangely enough, the large gray dog from that foreboding night in Turin began appearing on a regular basis to accompany the tireless priest home. Delighted to have a walking companion as formidable looking as the dog, Don Bosco decided to name his new friend Il Grigio, Italian for "The Gray One."

It wasn't long before Don Bosco learned Il Grigio was indeed as formidable as he looked.

One night Don Bosco was returning home late through a particularly bad section of Turin. He noticed two men nearby who seemed to be keeping pace with him. If he slowed down, they slowed down. If he sped up, they did the same. Finally, he crossed the street. When the men crossed also, the priest, certain now that they were after him, turned to run. But the two men caught him and threw a sack over his head.

They were attempting to gag him when suddenly growls like that of a bear or a wolf filled the air. Before the attackers could even see what was charging at them, Il Grigio lunged and seized one of the criminals by the neck. The luckier one ran off. The other, feeling Il Grigio's fangs around the tender flesh of his neck, pleaded with Don Bosco: "Call off your dog!"

Don Bosco heard the terrified man's pleas but was still a bit dazed from the attack. *My dog?* He shook his head clear and turned to face the robber.

"I will call him off, but next time leave strangers alone!"

"Yes! Yes! I will do anything, just please call him off!"

Before Don Bosco could say anything, the dog released the robber and trotted over to him. They stood together and watched the hapless thug flee down the darkened street.

It seemed to Don Bosco that Grigio had come into his life just when he needed him the most. Despite all the good he was doing, there were still those who wanted the priest out of the way. And some took a not-so-subtle approach.

One night, for instance, Don Bosco was walking down a familiar road when suddenly he found himself surrounded by a gang of twelve men armed with clubs. From out of nowhere, Grigio leapt into the group, growling fiercely. His menacing look was enough to make the attackers desist and run.

Sometimes Grigio would appear at Don Bosco's residence to take him to his destination. And at other times, the big dog would come into the house to prevent Don Bosco from going out. On one such occasion Grigio lay in front of the door and growled, warning the priest not to leave. The next day Don Bosco heard about a plan having been afoot to kill him.

After a period of time, the attacks and persecutions on Don Bosco occurred less frequently. The padre's admirers and benefactors eventually replaced in number his enemies, particularly as his reputation for holiness spread throughout Italy. He was no longer known just for working with troubled boys, but now for working genuine miracles. Healings, conversions, and mind reading were only some of the marvels that contributed to his celebrity.

Ten years passed without need of Grigio's assistance, but Don Bosco never forgot his faithful friend, nor did he stop wondering about him. Many questions remained in the priest's mind. Where did Grigio come from? Where did he go when he left? And what did he eat? (For no one ever saw the sturdy dog eat a single bite!)

Then one night Don Bosco was called to the home of a friend way out in the countryside. The road to the farmhouse was known to be dangerous, but Don Bosco could not disappoint a friend in need. He made his way along the dark and treacherous road, spying shadows behind every tree and hearing noises around every turn. Finally he sighed, "If only I had Grigio." No sooner did he utter the words than the big dog appeared at his side, looking the same as he did ten years ago and wagging his tail in unbridled joy.

After arriving safely at the farmhouse, Don Bosco ate dinner with the family while Grigio retired to a corner of the room. A little later the master of the house looked for Grigio in order to feed him, but the dog was nowhere to be found. Strangely enough, all the windows and doors remained firmly shut!

As Don Bosco grew older, he took great satisfaction in watching his work spread throughout the world. The small religious order he founded back in 1854 to take care of his burgeoning number of boys had grown steadily over the years. The Salesians (named after St. Francis de Sales) had spread to Spain, France, and South America. Never did a day go by that Don Bosco did not thank God for his good fortune.

Or for sending Grigio.

Don Bosco firmly believed that had it not been for the big gray dog, his work would have been severely hindered, if not stopped altogether. Asked once for his opinion about his furry friend's origin, Don Bosco replied, "It sounds ridiculous to call him an angel, yet he is no ordinary dog."

* * *

As jagged streaks of lightning emblazoned the angry sky, Don Bosco remembered his comment about Grigio. He was indeed no ordinary dog. But now it all seemed so long ago.

A crash of thunder stirred the elderly priest to attention. "We must keep going," he told his companion. "We need to find shelter."

"Father," replied the younger man, "I think we've strayed off the main road. This is some sort of swamp we're in."

Another flash of lightning lit up the sky and the men's surroundings. Nothing looked familiar. Don Bosco began to fear the worst: That they were lost in the stormy darkness!

Another flash. Wait! Something did look familiar. Could it be? Yes! Don Bosco shouted joyfully, "Grigio!"

The dog bounded over to the priests. His fur was as sleek as the first day Don Bosco saw him, and his magnificent form was as strong and healthy-looking as ever. It was as if time had stood still for The Gray One.

"Come," Don Bosco told the younger priest. "Follow the dog." He nodded toward Grigio, who was several paces ahead, waiting for the men to join him. Soon they arrived safely in the town. Then, as mysteriously as he had appeared, Grigio disappeared.

Later, the young priest asked Don Bosco, "Why did you call that dog Grigio? It surely couldn't have been the same dog you told me about."

"But it was, my son, it was my Grigio," Don Bosco replied with a knowing smile. "You saw for yourself how he came up to me to be petted. Just like he always did."

The saintly padre turned away, lost in thought. He knew that his last days on earth were drawing near. But he didn't mind. Indeed, he looked forward to that day when he would finally see, face to face, the God for whom he had toiled so hard.

And when he could once again see his beloved Il Grigio.

Il Grigio reportedly retained a fondness for the Salesians long after St. John Bosco left the world. Between 1893 and 1930, sisters of the Salesian order testified that they had received the gray dog's protection on at least three separate occasions.

ST. GEMMA GALGANI AND THE TEASING TASKMASTER

Why didn't Father see them? wondered Gemma. They were awfully hard to miss! The two marvelous winged creatures lit up the small room like lighthouse beacons.

Gemma wanted to shout out to Father Germano, but she held her tongue. She knew her luminous companions were sticklers for good behavior. No, shouting would not do at all.

Gemma focused as best she could on the kindly priest who sat beside her. She loved Father Germano. He had become so much more to her in these past months than just her confessor. He was her confidant and her friend. Gemma trusted him with her soul.

Father Germano, for his part, could read Gemma like a book.

"Daughter, what is it you keep looking at?" the priest asked.

"Oh, the angels, Father. Don't you see them? They are so beautiful. And yours has a brilliant star over his head. How can you not see them?"

Father Germano smiled at Gemma. Her simple, childlike faith never failed to inspire him. He had no doubt the young woman in his care was a saint. He prayed silently that he would counsel Gemma wisely.

"Gemma, you are very special. God has granted you a great privilege in being able to see and converse with your guardian angel."

Gemma looked at him quizzically. "You mean to say, Father, that most people don't know their angels?"

"Not like you, my dear," he said with a laugh. "Not like you."

She gazed up at the resplendent being standing attentively beside her. A shiver of sorrow raced through her fragile body at the thought of not being able to see him. For so long he had been comforting and teaching her, and even scolding her at times.

She silently thanked God for such a wonderful gift. Had her good angel not been constantly by her side, Gemma truly believed she would never have made it to this night.

* * *

Gemma was born on March 12, 1878, in the small Italian town of Camigliano. Even as a child, Gemma lovingly embraced the cross of Jesus. She would often take a crucifix from her mother's hands, clutch it tightly and kiss the sacred wounds.

Gemma was extremely devoted to her mother. When Mrs. Galgani became seriously ill shortly after Gemma's first confession, it nearly broke the young girl's heart. Gemma knew her mother was going to die. She kept a near-constant vigil at her bedside where the two of them often said the rosary together.

Yet when her mother finally succumbed to the illness that had plagued her for so long, it was Gemma who held up the rest of the family.

"Mother is in heaven," she constantly reminded her grieving brothers. "She is not suffering any longer."

Many more trials were soon to enter into Gemma's life. Not long after the death of her mother, she lost her brother Gino to another illness.

Her father died a few years later. At age nineteen, Gemma found herself orphaned and penniless. With nowhere else to go, Gemma moved in with her aunt, who soon began urging her attractive niece to marry. Gemma resisted. She had other plans.

For as long as she could remember, Gemma had wanted to become a Passionist nun. She was extremely devoted to St. Gabriel Possenti, a Passionist monk who had become her personal hero. Gemma's hopes to join St. Gabriel's order were dashed, however, when she became afflicted with spinal tuberculosis. The disease caused her much pain and left her practically paralyzed. She consoled herself during this difficult time by meditating on the passion of Jesus, and by praying diligently to St. Gabriel for strength. Gemma was more than willing to give her life to God if it was His will.

But a remarkable event occurred during the course of Gemma's illness. St. Gabriel appeared to Gemma one night and told her she would be cured. For the next several nights, St. Gabriel came to her bedside and prayed with her. Then, on a First Friday after receiving communion, Gemma felt Jesus asking her, "Gemma, do you wish to be cured?" Gemma was speechless, but in that instant she felt the cure take place in her body. Jesus then assured her that He had not abandoned her, even though the people she loved most on earth had been taken away.

* * *

Gemma blinked and focused on her current surroundings. Father Germano was looking at her patiently. The two angels were still present as well. Gemma likened them to two stars from heaven shining their light upon a small piece of earth. She met her own angel's gaze and could tell from his eyes that he had been sharing her memories with her.

Gemma, Jesus was always with you. He loves you so much he allowed you then, and allows you still, to share in His Passion. The angel's eyes flashed. *And I love you, too.*

Gemma's heart leapt with joy. She remembered that night a year ago when she came to realize just how much Jesus wanted her to follow in His footsteps . . .

61

* * *

On that night, June 8, 1899, Gemma had been deep in prayer when suddenly she felt a great pain in her hands and feet and side. With horror she saw that these parts of her body were dripping blood.

"Do not be afraid, Gemma," said her guardian angel. "Our Lord wishes you to suffer with Him for the sake of souls."

Shaken, but determined to bear her new cross with dignity, Gemma covered the wounds as best she could so as to not bleed on her clothing and bedcovers. Then, after her angel helped her into bed, she fell into a peaceful sleep.

As he had been that night, Gemma's guardian angel was nearly always visible to her. And on those infrequent occasions when he chose not to be, he was still very near. One day, the angel needed to remind Gemma of this fact.

Gemma was often the target of the devil's attacks because of her great holiness. Sometimes he would appear to her in some hideous form. At other times, he would attack by tempting her horribly with sins against purity. After one such struggle with temptation, which Gemma eventually overcame through persistent prayer, she was left feeling miserable and alone. Out of nowhere her angel appeared to her.

"Where have you been?" Gemma demanded. "Aren't you supposed to protect me at all times?"

The angel smiled while she continued to complain like a small child. He assured her that he had been with her throughout the attack and that he would always be with her, even if she could not see him.

"You withstood the evil one's snare in a manner most pleasing to God." Then the angel gently added, "You did nothing wrong, Gemma. Sin only occurs when you say yes to the temptation, not in the temptation itself."

As gentle and praising as her angel was with her in times of triumph, he could be stern and critical when Gemma did on occasion give in to temptations. Gemma wrote about one such occasion in her diary: "He ordered me to look in his face; I looked at him, but I soon lowered my eyes. He, however, insisted and said: 'Are you not ashamed to commit faults in my presence?'" Unable to bear the severe look her angel gave her, Gemma began to cry. She spent the rest of that day avoiding all eye contact with the angel, who continued to pierce her conscience with that scolding look.

To Gemma's great relief and delight, her angel never stayed angry with her for too long. Most of the time their relationship was more like brother and sister than parent and child. Hearing Gemma arguing one time with her angel, Father Germano urged Gemma to be more respectful. After all, she was talking to a blessed spirit! From that time on, Gemma was more careful with the way she spoke to her heavenly guardian.

A great deal of the time the angel instructed Gemma in spiritual matters, such as how she should conduct herself in daily life. Some of the lessons were challenging.

"Remember, daughter, that he who really loves Jesus talks little and bears everything. Never express your opinion if you are not requested to do so. Remember to watch over your eyes, and think that the eyes that have been mortified shall see the glories of heaven."

Heaven! Where her mother, father, and brother were waiting for her! Gemma needed to only think but a moment on that word to realize all her sufferings would soon pale in the backdrop of eternity. Father Germano was always reminding her of that. Father Germano, her dear spiritual director who had come to mean so much to Gemma. Father Germano!

Gemma suddenly remembered where she was and why. She was supposed to be telling Father about last night, and here she was daydreaming! When her eyes finally locked on Father's, she was relieved to see the same patient sparkle that she had come to know and love. Maybe she hadn't been reminiscing all that long.

With a glance toward the angels who still stood protectively beside their charges, Gemma began.

"Father, last night after my confession to Father Vallini . . . "

* * *

After Gemma returned home from confession, she sensed an evil presence around her. She began to pray. But no sooner had she started than the devil appeared to her in the form of a small, hideous creature. Alarmed, but knowing the devil could not harm her soul, Gemma continued to pray harder. Soon she began to feel actual blows on her shoulders! This lasted for nearly a half-hour. Suddenly her guardian angel appeared and the pummeling stopped.

"What is the matter?" he asked matter-of-factly.

"Oh please, dear angel, stay with me this night!" Gemma begged.

"But I need to sleep," he countered playfully.

Gemma knew better. "Angels of Jesus do not sleep!" she replied with indignation.

"Nevertheless, I ought to rest. Where shall you put me?"

Exhausted after her bout with the devil, and now this seemingly senseless banter, Gemma finally lay down in her bed. Tenderly, her angel spread his wings over her head and remained like that while she nodded off to sleep . . .

* * *

Looking lovingly at her angel, Gemma added, "And Father, he was still there this morning when I awoke, with his wings spread over me."

Father Germano stared at Gemma in awe. Not only did this child of God have the rare privilege of constantly seeing her angelic guardian, but she was on such a familiar basis with him that they teased each other like siblings!

Words failed the good priest at that moment. What could he possibly say? Finally, he instructed Gemma to write down everything that had happened last night in her diary, as he had been instructing her to do for more than a year. Then he prayed with her before leaving for the rectory. As he walked back he envisioned a brilliant angelic being with a star over its head striding beside him.

When his dear Gemma died three years later of tuberculosis on April 11, 1903, Father Germano tempered his grief with the firm belief that her soul arrived at the gates of Paradise at the very moment she took her last breath on earth.

He had little doubt that she entered on the wings of an angel.

The great war in heaven between St. Michael and the good angels and Lucifer and the bad angels ended happily. The good angels won! And they are on our side! Don't hesitate to call on your guardian angel whenever you feel tempted or fearful.

Remember this advice of St. John Bosco: "Ignore the devil and do not be afraid of him; he trembles and flees at your guardian angel's sight."

ST. PADRE PIO AND THE MESSENGERS OF THE 20TH CENTURY

Piergiorgio Biavati couldn't have been happier. He had gotten the day off from his car dealership in Florence and was on his way to San Giovanni to see Padre Pio. What luck, to have gained an audience with the famous stigmatic priest! Driving along the gorgeous "Highway of the Sun," Biavati sang along to his favorite radio station.

Suddenly he noticed the traffic slowing up all around him, until it came to a complete stop moments later. "Oh no," he muttered under his breath. *What a fine time for a traffic jam! What will Padre Pio think of me if I'm late?* For the next several hours Biavati crawled along the roadway. As the sun fell beneath the horizon, Biavati noted with frustration that he was only as far as Naples. He was supposed to be at the monastery by now!

Tired and upset, he pulled off the highway and stopped at a coffee shop. Better refuel for the three-hour drive ahead of me, he thought ruefully. After a short break, he got back into the car, ready to finish the journey. He turned the ignition key, heard the familiar sound of the starting engine, placed his hands on the steering wheel, and . . .

The next thing he remembered, someone was shaking him by the shoulder.

"Huh? Huh?" mumbled a groggy Biavati.

"Come on now, take over," said an unseen voice.

Biavati blinked several times and shook his head. He must have fallen asleep! He looked out at his surroundings. *How in the world?* He was at the friary! He looked at his watch. He had been sleeping for three hours! Bewildered, he went inside to seek Padre Pio.

At the risk of sounding like a lunatic, Biavati related his incredible story to the waiting Padre Pio. Though uncertain of the reaction the famed friar would have to his telling of the events, Biavati was nonetheless astonished at the reply he received. "You were right," Padre Pio stated matter-of-factly. "You were sleeping all the way and my guardian angel was driving for you."

* * *

Driving a car was only one of many tasks and favors Padre Pio's guardian angel performed for him. Moreover, such phenomena were not solely the work of one angel. Padre Pio talked and interacted not only with his own angel but also with other people's guardian angels like they were no different than the countless other visitors who daily came to see the famous priest. They were his constant companions. A fellow Capuchin and close friend of Padre Pio once remarked, "Padre Pio is in great cahoots with the angels."

If any soul in history deserved to be "in cahoots" with angels, it was the remarkable holy man from Pietrelcina, Italy. Born in 1887, Padre Pio is most famous for bearing the stigmata, the wounds of Jesus, for over fifty years. After joining the Capuchin order, Padre ("Father") Pio lived in the monastery at San Giovanni Rotondo. Although he rarely left the friary, he affected countless souls throughout the world by means of his prayers, advice, and example.

On June 16, 2002, Pope John Paul II canonized Padre Pio, no doubt with a great deal of personal joy and satisfaction. In 1962, when the Pope was a Cardinal in Krakow, Poland, he asked Padre Pio to pray for a Polish woman who was very sick. The woman was shortly thereafter cured, much to the amazement of attending doctors.

Padre Pio furthermore predicted that Cardinal Wojtyla would be elected Pope and would shed his blood during his pontificate. Could

Padre Pio have actually "seen" that day in 1981 when Pope John Paul II was seriously wounded by Mehmet Ali Agca's bullets?

Foretelling future events was just one of many supernatural gifts Padre Pio displayed while he was alive. The stigmata was his most visible and widely known charism. But he also had the ability to read people's minds and to know the condition of their souls; to be in two places at the same time; to convert sinners and unbelievers on the spot; to cure the sick; and, of course, to converse with angels.

What makes Padre Pio's angelic encounters so remarkable is the sheer number of witnesses—or, maybe a better word would be *participants*—who were involved. The saint did not just chat with his angel alone in his cell, but rather sent his angel all over the world for one reason or another. Sometimes the mission was to send a message; at other times the mission was more physical in nature, as in this story involving a very sleepy friar . . .

* * *

"If you want me to wake up, you'd better send in your guardian angel," Padre Paolino said to his friend, Padre Pio. Padre Pio had fallen ill, and Padre Paolino had offered to care for him through the night if he needed anything. But last night he hadn't heard Pio's calls for help. He was not surprised, for he was well aware of how deeply he slept.

He had thought about just moving into Padre Pio's room, but reconsidered. This would be the perfect opportunity to see for himself if Padre Pio's guardian angel was as reliable as his friend claimed. He went to bed the next night not quite knowing what to expect.

Around midnight, Padre Paolino felt himself awakened from a deep slumber. He looked around to see who had shaken him. But seeing no one in the room with him, and still quite tired, he fell back asleep. The following morning, Padre Paolino asked Padre Pio: "Why did your guardian angel let me go back to sleep last night? Tell him that if he comes tonight, he must make sure I get up."

That night, Padre Paolino again felt someone shake him awake in the middle of the night. But like the previous night, he fell back asleep almost instantly.

"Pio, tonight if you need me, have your angel wake me like he means it!" said Padre Paolino to his still sick friend the next day. "He must not let me have any peace until I get up."

On that third night, around 1:30 a.m., Padre Paolino was shaken awake once again. But this time he was practically pushed out of bed! He rushed to Padre Pio's bedside.

The sick, fever-ridden friar was drenched in sweat. And very glad to see Padre Paolino. "Please help me change my clothing. I can't do it alone," he said to his very wide-awake visitor.

Padre Paolino never felt the need to test Padre Pio's guardian angel again.

* * *

Padre Pio's reputation for holiness and unexplained phenomena attracted as much unwanted attention as that of the devout and sincere type. Knowing this, a friend of Padre Pio's, Padre Agostino, wrote him a letter in Greek in order to safeguard it from intruding eyes. Of course, Padre Agostino knew that Padre Pio didn't know Greek, but he also knew that Padre Pio was, at the time, living with a professor who did. Nonetheless, tongue in cheek, he wrote in the letter: "What will your angel say about this? God willing, your angel will be able to make you understand it. If not, write me."

Upon receiving the letter, Padre Pio dutifully took it to the professor. The professor was about to translate it for him when suddenly Padre Pio announced the entire contents of the letter, word for word!

The startled professor asked how he could possibly know what the letter said when he didn't even know the Greek alphabet.

"My guardian angel has explained everything to me," replied Padre Pio in customary short fashion.

After that, Padre Agostino sent Padre Pio letters in French, another language Padre Pio did not know. Yet the saintly friar had no difficulty reading the letters, and once even replied back in French.

"My little angel told me what to write," explained Padre Pio later.

Padre Pio's angel did not limit his translation services to written correspondence either. Many non-Italian speakers came away from Padre Pio's confessional shaking their heads, wondering how the holy priest had communicated with them perfectly when he knew no other languages but Italian. It was hard to accept Padre Pio's explanation: that his guardian angel did the interpreting!

* * *

Padre Pio frequently told his spiritual children to send their guardian angels to him whenever they needed his prayers but couldn't reach him in person. One group of followers discovered just how effective this advice could be when they found themselves in a rather desperate situation.

The pilgrims were on their way to San Giovanni Rotondo to see the world-famous stigmatic priest when their bus was caught in a sudden storm at night in the Apennine Mountains. They started to panic, for the storm was very fierce and they appeared to be quite alone in the wilderness.

"Everyone, listen!" shouted a young woman, trying to be heard above the fearful voices. "Remember what Padre Pio told us. Whenever we are in need of his prayers, we are to send our guardian angels to him."

They prayed earnestly: "Dear guardian angels, please ask Padre Pio to pray for us, that we might be delivered from harm."

A surprisingly short time later the storm subsided, and the bus made it to town without a scratch. The next morning the pilgrims were eager to tell Padre Pio about their adventure. But before they could utter a word, he smiled and answered their unspoken questions: "Well, my children, last night you woke me up and I had to pray for you."

* * *

Another of Padre Pio's friends, a young man from England, also discovered the reliability of this angelic messenger service. One day the young man was injured in a car accident. Another friend decided to telegraph the news to Padre Pio. When he arrived at the telegraph desk, however, he was startled to receive a telegram from Padre Pio first. The holy friar assured him in the telegram that he had prayed for his young friend's recovery.

When asked about the incident later, Padre Pio just smiled and said, "Do you think the angels go as slowly as the planes?"

* * *

It was not unusual for the monks at San Giovanni Rotondo to report strange or unusual happenings around the friary. Because many of the men had lived with Padre Pio for years and were accustomed to the supernatural phenomena that surrounded him, the thought that these incidents could be of celestial origin was hardly a leap of faith. The following story is yet another example . . .

"Surely those are not the voices of any of our friars!"

The younger priest looked at his superior and silently agreed. The singing was indeed exquisite, like nothing he had ever heard in the monastery, or beyond its walls for that matter. Where in the world was it coming from?

The two men continued to walk along the dimly lit corridors. From the faces of the other Capuchins they passed, they could tell they were not alone in hearing the wondrous harmony.

"Padre Alessio!" the superior called out upon catching sight of Padre Pio's confidant. Padre Alessio ambled over quickly.

"Do you hear that singing?" asked the superior.

"Yes. Isn't it beautiful?"

"Go and ask Padre Pio about this." The superior lowered his voice. "I have a feeling he might be able to clear up the mystery."

As Padre Alessio hurried off to Padre Pio's room, he couldn't help but think the superior was probably right. Anything this strange must have something to do with their distinguished resident friar.

He knocked softly on Padre Pio's door but received no answer. He opened the door and peeked inside. "Pio?" Still no answer. Then, looking around, he saw the priest sitting in a chair in the corner. He was still, as if asleep, yet his eyes were open, fixed on the crucifix on the wall.

"Pio?" asked Padre Alessio again.

Padre Pio jumped in his seat. "Huh?"

"Sorry to have bothered you, dear friend, but we are all wondering—"

"The singing?"

"Well, yes," replied Padre Alessio. "Do you know—?"

Padre Pio cut him off. "Why are you all so surprised? They are the voices of the angels, who are taking souls from purgatory into paradise."

* * *

The angels were undoubtedly singing on September 23, 1968, when Padre Pio passed from this world into theirs. Though it is not surprising that someone of Padre Pio's spiritual stature would have such an intimate relationship with the heavenly messengers, the saint himself believed that no one need be special or "holy" to recognize the doings of their own guardian angel.

They just needed to be looked for, he taught, with the eyes of faith.

Angels make perfect messengers because they are not limited by the laws of nature. In the time it takes to think up a message for your angel, he has already acted on it. In fact, angels themselves could be called "living thoughts," so swift is their method of motion.

Angels act in our best interest as messengers between God and us. How lovely is a prayer when brought to heaven by an angel. Remember always to ask your guardian angel to bring your needs and prayers to God. In return, he will bring you God's gifts and graces.

A WEEK WITH THE ANGELS

DEVOTIONAL SUGGESTIONS
FOR EVERY DAY

"Make friends with the holy angels," encouraged Pope St. Leo the Great.

What an easy instruction to follow! Our angels have already met us more than halfway. From the moment of our births, our guardian angels became our best, most loving, and faithful friends. And no matter how indifferent or negligent we are toward them, they will always do their very best to make us happy and holy.

Of course, there's no need to ignore our best friends when it is so easy to love them back. Here's one way to get started.

Take a week to try out the following thoughts and devotions. You'll like some better than others. And you may even think up some devotions of your own. After the week is over, keep up those activities and prayers that seemed to work best for you.

The result will be an eternity of friendship.

SUNDAY

Remember the Holy Angels at Mass

Before Mass, ask your guardian angel to help you in being attentive during the liturgy. Realize that you are in the presence of thousands of angels in church. St. Gregory tells us that at each Mass, "The Heavens open and the multitudes of angels come to assist at the Holy Sacrifice."

These are in addition to the guardian angels of everyone present in the church! St. Frances de Sales used to begin his sermons with a silent prayer to all of the guardian angels of the Mass-goers, asking them to make the hearts of the people more receptive to his words. After Mass, remember to say the Prayer to St. Michael to invoke his special protection for the Church.

Prayer to St. Michael the Archangel

St. Michael, the Archangel, defend us in battle. Be our protection against the wickedness and snares of the devil. May God rebuke him, we humbly pray. And do thou, O Prince of the Heavenly Hosts, by the power of God, cast into hell Satan and all evil spirits who prowl about the world seeking the ruin of souls. Amen.

MONDAY

Learn and Say Often the *Prayer to Your Guardian Angel*

> Angel of God
> My Guardian dear,
> To whom God's love
> Entrusts me here,
> Ever this day (or night)
> Be at my side,
> To light and guard
> To rule and guide.
> Amen.

Pope John XXIII was in the habit of saying this prayer five times a day! Don't hesitate to call upon your guardian angel for help whenever you face difficult tasks or choices. Your angel won't give you the answers to that tough exam, but if you ask, he'll calm you and help you remember things you already know.

TUESDAY

Celebrate "Angel Days"

The Church has traditionally devoted Tuesdays to the angels, just as it has devoted Saturdays to Mary, and Thursdays to the Blessed Sacrament. Do something special for your angel on Tuesday. Say some extra prayers of thanks. Set some time aside to talk with your angel. Or perhaps you're better at expressing yourself in writing.

Poetry is a wonderful way to offer praise, to give thanks, and to express your love. Many of the most popular books of the Bible are in poetry form, like the Psalms and Songs of Songs.

Many of the saints have written poems to honor their guardian angels. Here is a beautiful one from St. Therese of Lisieux:

To My Guardian Angel

O thou who speedest through all space
More swiftly than the lightnings fly,
Go very often in my place
To those I love most tenderly.

With thy soft touch, Oh, dry their tears,
Tell them the cross is sweet to bear,
Speak my name softly in their ears,
And Jesus' Name supremely fair!

The Church has also designated two days in its liturgical calendar just for angels: September 29th, the Feast of the Archangels Michael, Gabriel, and Raphael; and October 2nd, the Feast of the Guardian Angels. Mark your calendars and honor the angels on these special days. Attending Mass, in particular, is a wonderful way to say, "I love you."

WEDNESDAY

Send Your Angel Out to Others

St. Therese of Lisieux, though suffering herself with tuberculosis, often sent her angel out to console others in their pain or distress. Her poem above is an example of her charitable intentions.

With the quickness of a mere thought, it is possible to send a message of love and comfort to those we might not be able to see in person. When you have a good thought, or feel some joy in the midst of a bad spell, it might be someone else's angel delivering a message to you!

Just as we can ask our angels to go to those we love, we can also ask for their assistance in dealing with people who are difficult or don't like us.

Pope Pius XI made it a point before speaking to an adversary of asking his guardian angel to communicate with the angel of his opponent in order to soften that person's heart. "Once the two angels establish an understanding, the Pope's conversation with his visitors is much easier," the Pontiff explained one day to a Vatican diplomat.

Rather than get into a needless argument with someone you know to be disagreeable, ask your guardian angel to go on a "diplomatic mission" for you first.

THURSDAY

Greet the Guardian Angels of People You Meet During the Day

A silent good thought will do. There's no need to attract a lot of strange looks by talking to invisible beings. But think about it for a minute: Every person you pass on the street has a guardian angel at his or her side, just like you do. Why not send them a mental "hello" as you smile and greet their human partner?

In some parts of France many years ago, the custom of greeting other people's angels was quite common. It was not at all unusual to hear, "Good day, Sir, and your dear companion." Though this custom may have fallen out of fashion, there's no reason why we can't at least carry in our hearts and minds an awareness of the spiritual beings all around us.

FRIDAY

Remember the Guardian Angels When You Travel

We should of course ask for our own guardian angel's loving protection when we undertake any kind of journey, be it a trip to the store or a flight across the country.

But many Fathers of the Church believed that each place—for example, a city, a nation, a parish or a diocese—also has its own guardian angel, and that it is beneficial to pray to those angels when arriving at their location. St. Francis Xavier, the great sixteenth-century missionary, made it a habit of praying to the guardian angel of each foreign land he visited and asking for that angel's protection and help in preaching the Good News to the people there.

Prayer Before Starting a Journey

My holy angel guardian, ask the Lord to bless the journey which I undertake, that it may profit the health of my soul and body; that I may reach its end, and that, returning safe and sound, I may find my family in good health. Please guard, guide and preserve us. Amen.

SATURDAY

Read About the Angels

In order to honor and love our angels, we must first know them. This is accomplished most easily through reading. Be careful to choose books that are true to Church teachings and tradition. Many of the popular angel books out today teach about angels without any reference to Jesus Christ, the Commandments, or other Christian beliefs. A discussion about angels cannot take place without a discussion about God, too!

If you want to start right away, grab your Bible and read the Book of Tobit. It shouldn't take you too long to read this fascinating story about St. Raphael the Archangel and the help he rendered Tobit and his family.

MORE PRAYERS TO THE HOLY ANGELS

(From approved sources)

St. Gertrude's Guardian Angel Prayer

O most holy Angel of God, appointed by Him to be my guardian, I thank you for all the favors you have given me in body and soul. I praise and glorify you for assisting me with such patient fidelity, and for defending me against all the assaults of my enemies.

Blessed be the hour in which you were assigned to be my guardian, my defender, and my patron. In acknowledgment and return of all your loving ministries to me from my youth up, I offer you the infinitely precious and noble Heart of Jesus, and firmly resolve to obey you evermore, and most faithfully to serve my God. Amen.

Padre Pio's Guardian Angel Prayer

Angel of God,
my guardian,
to whom the goodness
of the Heavenly Father entrusts me.
Enlighten,
protect and guide me
Now and forever.
Amen.

Aspiration

O my dear Angel Guardian, preserve me from the misfortune of offending God.

Prayer of Praise

Father, in praising Your faithful angels and archangels, we also praise Your glory, for in honoring them, we honor You, their Creator. Their splendor shows us Your greatness, which surpasses in goodness the whole of creation. Amen.

Litany of the Holy Guardian Angel

Lord, have mercy on us.
Christ, have mercy on us.
Lord, have mercy on us.
Christ, hear us.
Christ, graciously hear us.
God the Father of heaven, have mercy on us.
God the Holy Spirit, have mercy on us.
Holy Trinity, one God, have mercy on us.

Holy Mary, Queen of Angels,   ["pray for us" after each line]
Holy Angel, my guardian,
Holy Angel, my prince,
Holy Angel, my monitor,
Holy Angel, my counselor
Holy Angel, my defender,
Holy Angel, my steward,
Holy Angel, friend
Holy Angel, my negotiator,

Holy Angel, my intercessor,
Holy Angel, my patron,
Holy Angel, director,
Holy Angel, my ruler
Holy Angel, my protector,
Holy Angel, my comforter,
Holy Angel, my brother,
Holy Angel, my teacher,
Holy Angel, my shepherd,
Holy Angel, my witness,
Holy Angel, my helper,
Holy Angel, my watcher,
Holy Angel, my conductor,
Holy Angel, my preserver,
Holy Angel, my instructor,
Holy Angel, my enlightener,

Lamb of God, who takes away the sins of the world, spare us, O Lord.
Lamb of God, who takes away the sins of the world, graciously hear us, O Lord.
Lamb of God, who takes away the sins of the world, have mercy on us.
Christ, hear us.
Christ, graciously hear us.
Lord, have mercy on us.

V. Pray for us, O holy Angel Guardian,
R. That we may be made worthy of the promises of Christ.

Let us pray: Almighty, everlasting God, who in the counsel of Thy ineffable goodness hast appointed to all the faithful, from their mother's womb, a special Angel Guardian of their body and soul;

grant that I may so love and honor him whom Thou has so mercifully given me, that, protected by the bounty of Thy grace and by his assistance, I may merit to behold, with him and all the Angelic hosts, the glory of Thy countenance in the heavenly kingdom. Who livest and reignest, world without end. Amen.

BIBLIOGRAPHY

Adels, Jill Haak. *The Wisdom of the Saints*. NY: Oxford University Press, 1987.

Attwater, Donald. *The Penguin Dictionary of Saints*. Middlesex, England: Penguin, 1965.

Austen, Rev. W.G., S.D.B. *Saint John Bosco*. London: Incorporated Catholic Truth Society, 1954.

Butler, Thurston, & Attwater. *Lives of the Saints*. (Complete Edition in 4 Volumes). Westminster, MD: Christian Classics, 1990.

Capes, F.M. *The Flower of the New World: A Short History of St. Rose of Lima*. London, England; R & T Washbourne, 1899.

The Catholic Encyclopedia, 1913 Edition.

Clarke, Catherine. *Our Glorious Popes*. Fitzwilliam, NH: Loreto Publications, 2000.

Danielou, Jean, S.J. *The Angels and Their Mission*, translated by David Heimann. Westminster, MD: Christian Classics, 1957.

De Sola Chervin, Ronda. *The Kiss from the Cross: Saints for Every Kind of Suffering*. Ann Arbor, MI: Servant Publications, 1994.

De Voragine, Jacobus, and William Granger Ryan (translator). *The Golden Legend*. Princeton, NJ: Princeton University Press, 1993.

Drahos, Mary. *Angels of God, Our Guardians Dear: Today's Catholics Rediscover Angels*. Ann Arbor, MI: Servant Publications, 1995.

Gheon, Henri. *Secrets of the Saints.* New York: Sheed & Ward, 1944.

Goodier, Alban, S.J. *Saints for Sinners.* New York: Image Books, 1959.

Habig, Rev. M.A., O.F.M. *Saints of the Americas.* Huntington, IN: Our Sunday Visitor, Inc., 1974.

Heffernan, Eileen, FSP. *Fifty-Seven Saints.* Boston: St. Paul Books & Media, 1994.

Hoagland, Victor, C.P. *The Book of Saints.* Farmingdale, NY: Regina Press, 1986.

Huber, Georges. *My Angel Will Go Before You*, translated by Michael Adams. Westminster, MD: Christian Classics, 1983.

Hughes, John Jay. *Pontiffs: Popes Who Shaped History.* Huntington, IN: Our Sunday Visitor, Inc., 1994.

Jovanovic, Pierre. *An Inquiry into the Existence of Guardian Angels: A Journalist's Investigative Report.* New York, NY: M. Evans and Company, Inc., 1995.

Kreeft, Peter J. *Angels and Demons: What Do We Really Know about Them?* San Francisco, CA: Ignatius Press, 1995.

Laux, Fr. John, M.A. *Church History.* Rockford, IL: Tan Books and Publishers, Inc., 1989.

Lord, Bob and Penny. *Heavenly Army of Angels.* Slidell, LA: Journeys of Faith, 1991.

Martindale, C.C., S.J. *The Queen's Daughters: A Study of Women*

Saints. New York: Sheed & Ward, 1951.

Matz, Terry. "Frances of Rome." Catholic Online Services, 1996.

O'Sullivan, Fr. Paul, O.P. *All About the Angels*. Rockford, IL: Tan Books and Publishers, Inc., 1990.

Paine, Rev. Randall, O.R.C. *The Angels are Waiting*. St. Paul, MN: Leaflet Missal Company, 1988.

Parente, Fr. Pascal P., S.T.D., Ph.D., J.C.B., *Beyond Space*. Rockford, IL: Tan Books and Publishers, Inc., 1973.

Ruffin, C. Bernard. *Padre Pio: The True Story*. Huntington, IN: Our Sunday Visitor, Inc., 1991.

St. Francis de Sales. *An Introduction to the Devout Life*. Rockford, IL: Tan Books and Publishers, Inc., 1994.

St. Michael and the Angels. Rockford, IL: Tan Books and Publishers, Inc., 1983.

St. Thomas Aquinas, *The Summa Theologica*, translated by the Fathers of the English Dominican Province. Benzinger Brothers, Inc., 1947.

Schouppe, Fr. F.X., S.J. *Purgatory: Explained by the Lives and Legends of the Saints*. Rockford, IL: Tan Books and Publishers, Inc., 1986.

Schug, Rev. John A., O.F.M. *A Padre Pio Profile*. Petersham, MA: St. Bede's Publications, 1987.

Steffon, Fr. Jeffrey. *Spiritual Warfare for Catholics*. Ann Arbor, MI: Servant Publications, 1994.

Thoughts of the Cure D' Ars. Rockford, IL: Tan Books, 1984.

ABOUT THE AUTHOR

Melaine Ryther is a freelance writer whose articles, essays and short stories have been published in a variety of print and online media outlets. Many of her works have appeared in Catholic publications, including *Columbia, Catholic Parent, Catholic Heritage, Catholic Digest,* and *The Liguorian*. She lives in Washington State with her husband and children.